THE BLOOD COVENANT

by

E. W. KENYON

(Compiled and Edited by
Ruth A. Kenyon)

32nd Printing

E.W. Kenyon
Author
(1867-1948)

Printed in U.S.A.

Copyright 1999
By
KENYON'S GOSPEL PUBLISHING SOCIETY
ISBN #1-57770-015-5

TABLE OF CONTENTS

FOREWORD

This subject opens an absolutely new field for research and study, for those who are deeply interested in obtaining the best and richest of God's provisions for man.

Those who have had the privilege of listening to Dr. Kenyon's lectures on this subject have long been asking that they might be put into print.

Until now, the way has not been opened whereby this might be done, but the time has at last come when the desire in the hearts of the people is to be granted.

The truth, hidden away in the memorial of the Lord's Table, and forming the foundation of it, is of such a nature that your heart will thrill in response to the possibilities that present themselves, and will stir you to lay hold on the same power and victory and miracles that became a part of the every day life of the apostles.

It is impossible to describe, in words, what the Blood Covenant will mean to you, once you learn what it is.

My father, Dr. E. W. Kenyon, the author of this manuscript, went home to be with His Lord, March 19, 1948, but the work which he started is still going on and blessing countless thousands.

This book is being printed as a lasting memorial to him, and has been made possible by the love gifts of those who have been helped and blessed by his ministry.

RUTH A. KENYON

Chapter One

THE NEW COVENANT IN MY BLOOD

For years, I was convinced that there was something in the Lord's Table that I did not understand.

The silence of the disciples when Jesus introduced it, saying "This is my blood of the New Covenant, which is poured out for many unto the remission of sins"; and then told them to eat the bread which was His body and to drink the wine which He declared was His blood,—I say, the very silence of the disciples indicates they understood what he meant.

I did not, and it confused me.

For a long time I asked the question, "What is the underlying principle involved in this strange ordinance?"

The very language of Jesus, when He said, "Verily, verily, I say unto you, except ye eat of the flesh of the son of man, and drink His blood, ye have not life in yourselves," added to the confusion.

What did He mean by it?

Then, there was placed in my hands a book by Dr. H. Clay Trumbull, the old editor of the Sunday School Times, in which he showed there had been a Blood Covenant practiced by all primitive peoples from time immemorial.

He proved that this Blood Covenant was the basis of all primitive religions.

He gave data from all parts of the world showing that even to this day, in Africa, India, China, Borneo, and the Islands of the Seas, men are practicing a Blood Covenant very similar to our Lord's Table.

It was degenerated, but never-the-less, it had the marks of an original revelation from God.

In Stanley's books of exploration in Africa, he tells us that he cut the Covenant more than fifty times with different tribes.

Livingstone calls attention to it, as do other explorers and missionaries in Africa.

Perhaps it might help us to understand if we look at the Hebrew word for Covenant.

It means "to cut." It has the suggestion of an incision where blood flows.

In practically every place where the word is used in the Scripture, it means "to cut the Covenant."

We find that Abraham "cut the Covenant" with some of his neighbors before he ever entered into the Covenant with Jehovah.

Chapter Two

THE ORIGIN OF THE BLOOD COVENANT

The Blood Covenant, or what we call the Lord's Table, is based upon the oldest known covenant in the human family.

It evidently began in the Garden of Eden.

It is evident that God cut the covenant or entered into a covenant with Adam at the very beginning.

The reason I believe that, is because there isn't a primitive people in the world, as far as we know, that has not practiced the blood covenant in some form; showing that it had a God given origin and so man has practiced the covenant through all the ages.

Today, hundreds of tribes in equatorial Africa cut the covenant.

Stanley cut the covenant fifty times with different tribes.

Livingstone cut the covenant.

Missionaries have seen it enacted, but didn't understand the significance, thinking it was some heathen rite, and not realizing that the blood covenant practiced in Africa today would open the doors in every tribe for the Gospel of the Lord Jesus Christ.

If any missionary who understands the language of any of the tribes would explain to them the Lord's Table and let them see what it meant, out of what it grew, it would at once open the door to the Gospel to them.

The whole Redemptive plan swings about the Two Covenants.

You remember, we have an Old Covenant and a New Covenant.

Perhaps I had better illustrate to you what this ancient Covenant means, because it is practically the same among all peoples.

REASONS FOR CUTTING THE COVENANT

There are three reasons for men cutting the covenant with each other.

If a strong tribe lives by the side of a weaker tribe, and there is danger of the weaker tribe being destroyed, the weaker tribe will seek to "cut the Covenant" with the stronger tribe that they may be preserved.

Second, two business men entering into a partnership might cut the Covenant to insure that neither would take advantage of the other.

Third, if two men loved each other as devotedly as David and Jonathan, or as Damon and Pythias, they would cut the Covenant for that love's sake.

THE METHOD OF CUTTING THE COVENANT

The method of cutting the covenant is practically the same the world over; although there are differences of course.

In some places it has degenerated into a very grotesque, almost a horrible rite, but nevertheless it is the same blood covenant.

That which is practiced by the native tribes of Africa, by the Arabs, by the Syrians, and by the Balkans is this:

Two men wish to cut the covenant; they come together with their friends and a priest.

First, they exchange gifts. By this exchange of gifts they indicate that all that one has the other owns if necessary.

After the exchange of gifts, they bring a cup of wine, the priest makes an incision in the arm of one man and the blood drips into the wine.

An incision is made in the other man's arm and his blood drips into the same cup.

Then the wine is stirred and the bloods are mixed. Then the cup is handed to one man and he drinks part of it, then hands it to the other man and he drinks the rest of it.

When they have drunk it, ofttimes they will put their wrists together so that their bloods mingle, or they will touch their tongues to each other's wounds.

Now, they have become blood brothers.

THE SACREDNESS OF THE BLOOD COVENANT

Mr. Stanley said he never knew this covenant to be broken in Africa, no matter what the provocation.

Dr. Livingstone also bears witness saying that he never knew it to be broken.

In other parts of the world it is claimed that they never knew the Blood Covenant to be broken.

It is one covenant that is perfectly sacred among all primitive peoples.

In Africa, if one was to break the covenant, his own mother or wife, or his nearest relatives would seek his death, would turn him over to the hands of the avenger for destruction. No man can live in Africa who breaks the covenant . . . he curses the very ground he walks on.

The vilest enemies become trusted friends as soon as the covenant is cut.

No man takes advantage of the covenant or breaks it.

It is so sacred that the children to the third and fourth generations revere it and keep it.

In other words, it is a perpetual covenant, indissoluble, a covenant that cannot be annulled.

Chapter Three

THE COVENANT IN AFRICA

One illustration of Stanley's might help us to grasp the significance.

When Stanley was seeking Livingstone, he came in contact with a powerful equatorial tribe. They were very war-like.

Stanley was not in condition to fight them.

Finally, his interpreter asked him why he didn't make a strong covenant with them.

He asked what it meant and was told that it meant drinking each other's blood.

Stanley revolted from such a rite, but conditions kept growing worse, until finally the young colored man asked him again why he did not cut the covenant with the chieftain of the tribe.

Stanley asked what the results of such a covenant would be, and the interpreter answered. "Everything the chieftain has will be yours if you need it."

This appealed to Stanley and he investigated.

After several days of negotiation, they arrived at the covenant.

First, there was a parley in which the chieftain questioned Stanley as to his motives and standing, and his ability to keep the covenant.

The next step was an exchange of gifts.

The old chieftain wanted Stanley's new white goat.

Stanley was in poor health and goat's milk was about all he could take for nourishment, so it was very hard for him to give this up, but the chieftain seemed to want nothing else.

So he finally gave up the goat, and the old chieftain handed him his seven-foot copper-wound spear.

Stanley thought he had been beaten, but he found that wherever he went in Africa with that spear, everybody bowed to him and submitted to him.

The old chieftain then brought in one of his princes.

Stanley led forth one of his men, from England.

Then the priest came forward with a cup of wine, made an incision in the young black's wrist, and let the blood drip into the cup of wine. He cut a like incision in the wrist of the young Englishman, and let his blood also drip into the cup of wine.

Then the wine was stirred and the bloods were mixed.

The priest handed the cup to the Englishman and he drank part of it and then handed it to the black and he drank the rest of it.

Next, they rubbed their wrists together so that their bloods mingled.

Now, they had become blood brothers.

These two men were only substitutes, but they had bound Stanley and the chieftain, and Stanley's men and the chieftain's soldiers into a blood brotherhood that was indissoluble.

Then gun-powder was rubbed into the wound, so that when it healed there would be a black mark to indicate that they were covenant men.

The next step in this ceremony was the planting of trees, trees that were known for their long life.

After the planting of the trees, then the chieftain stepped forward and shouted, "Come, buy and sell with Stanley, for he is our blood brother."

A few hours before, Stanley's men had to stand on guard about their bales of cotton cloth and trinkets, but now he could open the bales and leave them on the street and nothing was disturbed.

For anyone to steal from their blood brother, Stanley, was a death penalty.

The old chieftain couldn't do enough for his new found brother.

Stanley couldn't understand the sacredness of it, and years later wondered about it.

CURSES AND BLESSINGS

I have left out a very important feature of this ceremony.

As soon as the two young men had drunk each other's blood, a priest stepped out and pronounced the most awful curses that Stanley had ever heard; curses that were to come upon him if he broke the covenant.

Then Stanley's interpreter took his part and pronounced curses upon the old king, his wife, his children and his tribe, if they broke the covenant with Stanley.

You remember, when Moses apportioned the land to the different tribes, he called their attention to the mountain of cursing and the mountain of blessing?

In Deut. 11th and 27th Chapters, you find the curses of the Old Covenant and the blessings of the Covenant.

The curses were pronounced from the mount of cursing

each year, and the blessings were pronounced from the mount of blessing each year.

THE MEMORIAL

The ceremony of tree planting was always done, if they were in a country where trees grow.

These are called memorial trees, Trees of the Covenant.

In a place where trees do not grow, they set up a pile of stones or erect a monument as a memorial to remind them and their descendants that they are partners in an indissoluble covenant.

You remember Abraham gave to Abimelech some ewe lambs, and the lambs were for a memorial.

As the lambs grew and the flocks grew, that flock would be a continual reminder of the Covenant that had been cut.

The moment a covenant is solemnized, everything that a blood covenant man owns in the world is at the disposal of his blood brother if he needs it, and yet this brother would never ask for anything unless he were absolutely driven by want to do it.

Some of the most beautiful stories I know in the world are the stories of blood covenant brothers.

Another feature of this is, that as soon as they cut the covenant, they are recognized as blood brothers by others, and they are called the blood brothers.

Chapter Four

JEHOVAH CUTS THE COVENANT WITH ABRAHAM

When God entered into the covenant with Abraham, there were several very striking events that took place.

Among them was the changing of Abram's and Sarai's names to Abraham (a prince of God) and Sarah (princess of God.)

In other words, He lifted them into the royal family before He cut the Covenant with them.

The Abrahamic Covenant which is the basis of Judaism and Christianity is the most marvelous document in existence.

It was sealed by circumcision. Gen. 17.

This covenant bound Abraham and his descendants by indissoluble ties to Jehovah, and it bound Jehovah to Abraham and his descendants by the same solemn token.

THE CUTTING OF THE COVENANT

When Abraham was 99 years of age, God appeared to him as "God Almighty" or "El Shaddai."

He said unto Abraham, "Walk before me and be thou perfect. And I will make my covenant between me and thee, and will multiply thee exceedingly."

We see Abraham on his face. God is talking with him. God tells him, "As for me, behold, my covenant is with thee, and thou shalt be the father of a multitude of nations. Neither shall thy name any more be called Abram, but thy name shall be Abraham, for the father of a multitude of nations have I made thee."

In Genesis 15:6, God made a promise to Abraham and it says that "Abraham believed God and it was reckoned to him for righteousness."

This word "believe" means that Abraham made an "Unqualified committal" of himself and all he was or ever would be, to God.

The word "believe" here in the Hebrew means not only a "loving trust," but it also means "give yourself wholly up," or, "to be a part of Himself," or "go right into him," or "the unqualified committal."

Abraham gave himself to God in utter abandonment of self.

On the ground of that, God said, "Take for me," that is, as God's substitute, "an animal and slay it."

Abraham did it.

Then God said, "My substitute has been slain, and I want you to circumcise yourself," so that his blood would mingle with the blood of God's substitute.

When that was done, God and Abraham had entered the Covenant.

It meant that all Abraham had or ever would have was laid on the altar.

It meant that God must sustain and protect Abraham to the very limit.

When God cut the Covenant with Abraham the Israelitish nation came into being as a Covenant People because of this Covenant.

This Covenant was limited to Israel, the children of Abraham, and had behind it the Promise and the Oath of God. Gen. 22:16-18.

SOME COVENANT FACTS

The Seal of the Covenant was circumcision.

Every male child at eight days of age was circumcised, and the circumcision was the entrance into the Abrahamic Covenant.

When that child was circumcised, entered into the Covenant, then that child became an inheritor of everything connected with the Covenant.

If the child's father and mother should die, another Israelite is under obligation to care for the child; or if the husband should die, to care for the widow. It is the Law of the Covenant.

All things are laid upon the altar of this Covenant.

If keeping the Covenant with a blood brother meant the death or loss of wife, or of first born, or the destruction of his property, or of his own life, all, everything was laid upon the altar.

THE COVENANT OBLIGATIONS

Gen. 17:13, "And my covenant shall be in your flesh for an everlasting Covenant."

Every male child at eight days of age was circumcised. This mark on their bodies was the seal of their place in the Covenant, and as long as Israel kept this Covenant that was renewed in Moses, there weren't enemies enough in the whole world to conquer one little village.

When God led Israel out of Egypt by Moses they had no law, no priesthood.

Then God gave them the ten commandments, the priesthood, the Atonement, the sacrifices, the offerings, and the laws that govern the sacrifices and the offerings, the scape-goat, and the worship. All these belonged to the Covenant.

The Covenant did not belong to the ten commandments as modernists put it, but the Covenant was the reason for the Law.

It was called the law of the Covenant.

Israel were the people of the Covenant.

Read Ex. and Lev. carefully, noting when the word "Atonement" first occurs, when the law was given, when the priesthood was set apart.

Study Lev. 16 and 17 carefully. Note what the blood meant, and the significance of the word "Atonement."

Chapter Five

ABRAHAM'S SACRIFICE

"Take now thy son, thine only son, whom thou lovest. . ."

You know the rest of that fearful command that came to the man, Abraham, as he stood transfixed in the presence of the angel of the Covenant.

There was no wavering on the part of Abraham.

Consider what this meant to him. We know how he had hungered for a son.

We know how he expressed his longings to Jehovah, in those years when it seemed that such a possibility was gone forever.

Then Jehovah promised him a son.

Gen. 17:15-17, "And God said unto Abraham, As for Sarai, thy wife, thou shalt not call her name Sarai, but Sarah shall her name be. And I will bless her, and moreover I will give thee a son of her: yea I will bless her, and she shall be a mother of nations; kings of peoples shall be of her. Then Abraham fell upon his face, and laughed, and said in his heart, Shall a child be born unto him that is a hundred years old? and shall Sarah, that is ninety years old, bear?

" . . . And God said, . . . Sarah thy wife shall bear thee a son; and thou shalt call his name Isaac: and I will establish my covenant with him for an everlasting covenant for his seed after him." Gen. 17:19.

Abraham and Sarah were old. Abraham was nearly a hundred years old, and Sarah was ninety. In the realm of the senses for them to become the parents of a child was impossible, for the scripture tells us in Gen. 18:11, "Now

Abraham and Sarah were old, and well stricken in age; it had ceased to be with Sarah after the manner of women."

But Abraham considered not his own body, which was as good as dead, nor the deadness of Sarah's womb, but looking unto God, he waxed strong.

He counted that God was able to make good anything that He promised. The Scripture tells us, "Abraham believed God."

Gen. 21:1-3, "And Jehovah visited Sarah as he had said, and Jehovah did unto Sarah as he had spoken. And Sarah conceived, and bare Abraham a son in his old age . . . And Abraham called the name of his son Isaac (which means laughter)."

The child grew to be 18 or 20 years of age; then God asked for the boy.

He said: "Take now thy son, thine only son, even Isaac, whom thou lovest unto a mountain which I will show thee and offer him there as a burnt offering." Gen. 22:2.

Abraham did not hesitate, though it meant giving up all he held dear, but took the young man on that three days and three nights journey.

They arrived at Mt. Moriah and together they built the altar.

Abraham laid the young man on the altar and drew the knife to slay him, when the Angel of the Lord shouted to him, saying, "Abraham! Abraham! stay thy hand."

God had found a man that would keep the Covenant; He had found a covenant-keeping man.

Now hear what God said: "By Myself have I sworn," saith Jehovah, "for because thou hast done this thing, and hast not withheld thy son, thine only son; that in blessing I will bless thee, and in multiplying I will multiply thy seed as the stars of the heaven." Gen. 22:16, 17.

Did you notice, "By myself have I sworn." God's throne became the surety of His promise.

It is the most solemn thing that a man can conceive.

Abraham had proved his worthiness of God's confidence.

THE COVENANT KEEPING GOD

You remember that before this thing happened, when God was going to destroy Sodom and Gomorrah, He said it wasn't best to do it without talking it over with Abraham.

You remember Abraham's great appeal and how he talked with God in a manner that would stagger one.

He said, "Will not the God of all earth do right?"

Then he began to plead for the righteous ones in those cities, and God permitted that man on the ground of his Blood Covenant relationship to become the intercessor for the wicked cities of Sodom and Gomorrah.

When Abraham entered into the Covenant, he gained the right to arbitrate between the wicked men of the earth and the God of the whole earth.

Abraham established a blood-covenant precedent of intercession that has stood through all the ages.

Chapter Six

THE ABRAHAMIC COVENANT

The Abrahamic Covenant was the reason for Israel's being.

There would have been no nation, had God not given them the Covenant.

You remember that Isaac was born after Abraham was one hundred years old, and Sarah was past ninety years old.

Isaac, father of the Israelitish nation was a miracle child.

That nation went down into Egypt, after Isaac's grandchildren had grown to manhood. They were delivered out of Egypt, 400 years later, after having served in bondage for over 300 years.

No nation had ever been delivered like that. It was the rarest, most unique national experience in history.

They were delivered because they were God's Blood Covenant people.

In Exodus 2, when God heard the groanings of Israel in Egypt, He said that He remembered His Covenant that He had made with Abraham, Isaac and Jacob.

God sent Moses down into Egypt to deliver Abraham's Blood Covenant descendants.

God couldn't break the Covenant. He could not forget it nor ignore it.

He is the covenant-keeping God.

Back behind Israel was this solemn Covenant that God had sealed on His side, by putting Himself in utter, absolute bondage to that Covenant.

God and Israel were bound together.

As long as Israel kept the Covenant there were no sick people among the Israelites.

When He said, "I am Jehovah that healeth thee," that settled it.

Jehovah was their only physician.

He was not only their physician, but He was their succor, He was their protector.

There was never a barren wife, no babies ever died, no young men and women ever died unless they broke the Covenant.

As long as they kept the Covenant, there were not allied armies enough in the world to conquer one little village.

In battle, no soldiers were slain.

They were Blood-Covenant men.

Moses led them out of Egypt into a barren desert . . . comparable to our own Mojave desert . . . and on the ground of the Covenant, God supplied them with water for themselves and their cattle, and manna for the people.

When they came out of Egypt, it was through signs and wonders that staggered the whole world at the time, and have been the wonder and amazement of the world ever since.

God preserved them as a nation because they were His Covenant people.

When they sinned and broke the Covenant, they were carried away into captivity and into Babylon.

They had sinned against the Covenant. They had brought Judgment upon themselves.

But, in the face of that, God remembered the Covenant He had made with Abraham years before. They were given a Revelation of God.

We call it the Old Covenant; we call it the Law of the Prophets and the Psalms.

Israel was given this Revelation of God and this Law of God because they were God's Blood Covenant people.

Then, later, God gave them Jesus because they were the Blood Covenant people.

Jesus became the founder of the New Covenant. We have that New Covenant, because they had the Abrahamic Covenant.

We enter into the strange blessings that they entered into, and richer, because of the New Covenant of which Jesus is the surety.

Chapter Seven

ISRAEL, THE BLOOD COVENANT PEOPLE

I want to call your attention to several miracle things in connection with Israel, the Blood Covenant people.

This Covenant guaranteed to them physical protection... protection from their enemies, from the pestilence and from diseases.

They went into Egypt and became a great nation of over three million people. God brought them forth by a series of miracles that absolutely stagger the human reason.

He did this because He was in Blood Covenant relationship with Israel, and was under bond to deliver them.

As they stood on the shore of the Red Sea, after they had been delivered from their bondage, God said: "I am the Lord that healeth thee."

Then He promised them that none of the diseases of the Egyptians should come upon them.

He was their Blood Covenant Physician. We can hardly grasp this.

We know that for forty years they wandered in the desert land.

God gave them the cloud for protection from that fierce desert sun, and at night he gave them the pillar of fire for light and heat.

God gave them food and water. He met their every need.

THE LAW AND THE PRIESTHOOD

Then God gave them the Blood Covenant Law. We call it the Mosaic Law, because Moses was the instrument through which it came to Israel.

This law was to separate them from all other peoples of the earth. It was to make them a peculiar people on whom God could bestow unusual blessings, and it was on the basis of the Blood Covenant.

The Covenant was the center around which all of Israel's life moved.

After the giving of the Law, the Law was broken. A priesthood was imperative.

There had never been a divinely appointed priesthood in the human race before, but now God appointed the Priesthood and the High Priest.

With the Priesthood were given the Atonement Offerings. Never before had there been an Atonement Offering or the Great Day of Atonement.

All the offerings they had known had been the Peace Offerings or the whole Burnt Offering.

Now God appointed a special sacrifice in which the blood was to cover the broken Law, and cover spiritually dead Israel so that God could dwell in their midst.

The word "atonement" in the Hebrew means to cover, and God gave it because of the life that was in the blood, and that life in the blood served as a covering for spiritually dead Israel and its broken Law, and Israel's unfitness to stand uncovered in the presence of God.

The Blood Covenant Priesthood headed up in the High

Priest. He became the surety of the Covenant. He stood between the people and God.

Once a year He entered into the Holy of Holies to make the yearly Atonement.

This was the only time the High Priest ever functioned, unless some grievous sin broke out among the people.

The High Priest's function was peculiar in that once a year He made the Covering or Atonement for the people, and confessed the sins of the people on the head of the scapegoat, and then sent him out in the wilderness to be destroyed.

His presence was necessary to maintain their fellowship and insure their protection.

With the Atonement and the Priesthood, came the Blood Covenant sacrifices.

The five great offerings mentioned in the first seven chapters of Leviticus were the Whole Burnt Offering, the Meal Offering, the Peace Offering, the Trespass Offering, and the Sin Offering.

These offerings were fellowship offerings and broken fellowship offerings.

They had to do with the daily life of the people.

When an Israelite was in fellowship, he could bring the Whole Burnt Offering, or the Meal or Peace Offering.

When he had sinned against his brother, he could bring the Trespass Offering.

When he had sinned against the Holy things of God, he brought the Sin Offering.

In this last, the High Priest under certain conditions officiated.

They were Blood Covenant People and must be kept in fellowship with the Blood Covenant obligations and privileges.

BLESSINGS OF THE COVENANT

God was under obligation to shield them from the armies of the nations that surrounded them.

God was under obligation to see that their land brought forth large crops.

God was under obligation by the covenant to see that the herds and flocks multiplied.

The hand of God was upon them in blessing.

They became the head of the nations and of wealth.

Jerusalem became the richest city the world had ever known.

Their hillsides were irrigated, their valleys teemed with wealth.

There was no city like it, no nation like it.

God was their God, they were God's Covenant people.

Under the Covenant one man could chase a thousand in war, and two could put ten thousand to flight.

In David's day when Covenant truth became a living force in the nation, David had Blood Covenant warriors that could individually slay eight hundred men in a single combat.

They could without weapons rend a lion as though it had been a kid.

They had physical strength and prowess. They had divine protection that made them the greatest warriors the world ever knew.

They were God's peculiar people. They were the treasure of the heart of God.

THE JUDGMENT

There isn't a more tragic event in human history than the destruction of the city of Jerusalem, and the carrying away of the people into Babylon because they had sinned against the Covenant.

The heavens became brass, the earth as iron, their rain was turned to dust; diseases afflicted them; enemies overran them, until their great city, the richest city the world had ever known, was but a heap of ruins. The temple which cost more money than any other ever reared was completely destroyed and lay in dust and ashes.

They had broken the Covenant.

Chapter Eight

THE NEW COVENANT

Now then, we have a background.

We come to the New Testament, and see Jesus and the disciples gathered together that night before the Crucifixion.

Jesus said, "I long to break this bread with you and drink this cup"; and after He had blessed the bread and brake it, He said, "This is My body that is broken for you." Then He took a cup of wine and said, "This is My Blood of the New Covenant that is poured out for many unto the remission of sins."

The old Blood Covenant was the basis on which the New Covenant was founded.

Now you can understand that when Jesus said, "This is my blood of the New Covenant," the disciples knew what it meant. They knew that when they cut the Covenant with Jesus in that upper room that night, they had entered into the strongest, most sacred Covenant known to the human heart.

JESUS, THE SURETY

Jesus brings us a New Covenant, having displaced and fulfilled the Old Covenant. Heb. 10:9.

With the fulfilling of the Old Covenant, everything connected with it was set aside.

As the Old Covenant was sealed with circumcision, the New Covenant is sealed with the New Birth.

The Old Covenant had the Levitical Priesthood.

The New Covenant has Jesus as the High Priest, and we as the royal and Holy Priesthood. 1 Pet. 2:1-10.

The first priesthood had a temple in which God dwelt in the Holy of Holies with the Ark of the Covenant. Ex. 40.

In the New Covenant our bodies are the temple of God, and the Spirit dwells within them.

Jehovah was the Surety of the Old Covenant.

Heb. 7:22, "By so much also hath Jesus become the Surety of a better covenant."

Jesus stands back of every sentence in the New Covenant.

He is the great Intercessor of the New Covenant. "He is able to save all that come unto God by Him, seeing He ever liveth to make intercession for them." Heb. 7:25.

God bound Himself with an oath to the Old Covenant. He was the surety of the Old Covenant. He said, "By Myself have I sworn."

Just as God stood behind the Old Covenant and was its surety, so Jesus is the Surety of every Word in the New.

What strong faith should be builded upon a foundation like this.

The resources of Heaven are back of Jesus and back of that Covenant.

Chapter Nine

CONTRAST OF THE TWO COVENANTS

The Bible is composed of two covenants, contracts or agreements.

The first covenant was between Abraham and Jehovah. It was sealed by circumcision. Gen. 17.

It is often called the "Law Covenant" or the "Mosaic Covenant." Both titles are wrong.

It is the Abrahamic Covenant, and the Law that was given through Moses belonged to the Covenant.

When the Israelites were delivered from Egypt, they had no law, nor government, so Jehovah gave them the law.

We call it the Mosaic Law. Ex. 20.

It is the Covenant Law, with its priesthood, sacrifices, ceremonies and offerings.

The law had no sooner been given than it was broken. Then God provided the Atonement (or covering) for the broken law. Ex. 24.

The word "Atonement" means "to cover." It is not a New Testament word, it does not appear in the New Testament Greek.

Why?

Because the blood of Jesus Christ cleanses, instead of merely covering.

The first covenant did not take away sin, it merely covered it.

It did not give Eternal Life or the New Birth. It gave a promise of it.

It did not give Fellowship with God. It gave a type of it.

It gave protection to Israel as a nation, it met their physical needs.

God was Israel's Healer, Provider, and Protector.

You cannot separate Moses' Law from the Covenant, so when the Covenant was fulfilled, the Law was fulfilled and set aside.

Heb. 10:1, "For the law having a shadow of the good things to come, not the very image of the things, can never with the same sacrifices year by year, which they offer continually, make perfect them that draw nigh."

All that Law and the First Covenant was a shadow.

The sacrifices could never make perfect the man under the Covenant, "Else would they not have ceased to be offered? because the worshippers, having once been cleansed, would have no more consciousness of sins."

The blood of bulls and goats did not cleanse the conscience, did not take away sin consciousness from man.

The inference is that there is a sacrifice that takes away the sin consciousness so that man stands uncondemned in God's presence.

Rom. 8:1, "There is therefore now no condemnation to them that are in Christ Jesus."

Rom. 5:1, "Being therefore justified by faith, we have peace with God through our Lord Jesus Christ."

Rom. 3:26, God becomes our Righteousness or our Justification, "That He might Himself be Righteous, and the Righteousness of him that hath faith in Jesus."

The First Covenant was sealed by the blood of Abraham, and God sacrificed an animal.

This New Covenant is sealed with the blood of Jesus Christ, God's own Son.

Heb. 8:1, "We have such a high priest, who sat down on the right hand of the throne of the Majesty in the heavens."

He is the minister of the true tabernacle which the Lord prepared instead of Moses.

Everything centered around the High Priest under the Old Covenant. When the High Priest failed, the people had no approach to God.

Everything centers around our New High Priest under the New Covenant, but our High Priest can never fail His people.

"But now hath He obtained a ministry the more excellent, by so much as He is also the Mediator of a better covenant which hath been enacted upon better promises."

The High Priest was an earthly mediator between Israel and Jehovah. Jesus is the Mediator of the New Covenant.

Chapter Ten

A STUDY IN HEBREWS

The book of Hebrews has several vital contrasts.

There is the contrast of Moses and Jesus; of Aaron, the High Priest, and Jesus the New High Priest; and the contrast of the blood of bulls and goats and the blood of Christ.

It is not only a contrast of the bloods, but of the two tabernacles . . . the one reared by Moses and the one in Heaven. Into this latter one Jesus enters, and sits down there as our High Priest.

His home is the Holy of Holies.

The Priest under the Old Covenant could only stay long enough to make the Atonement.

Heb. 9:21-23 tells how the tabernacle and all the vessels were cleansed with blood.

"Moreover the tabernacle and all the vessels of the ministry he sprinkled in like manner with the blood. And according to the law, I may almost say, all things are cleansed with blood, and apart from shedding of blood there is no remission. It was necessary therefore that the copies of the things in the heavens should be cleansed with these; but the heavenly things themselves with better sacrifices than these."

This is a startling thing, but Adam's sin had touched heaven itself.

The 24th verse, "For Christ entered not into a holy place made with hands, like in pattern to the true; but into heaven itself, now to appear before the face of God for us."

This is the climax of it all.

This lets us see the contrast of God's estimation of the blood of Christ and the blood of bulls and goats.

As we come to value the blood of Christ as God values it, then the problem of our standing and relationship never enters our minds.

THE NEW MEDIATOR

The blood of bulls and goats, under the first Covenant, only cleansed or sanctified the flesh, but the blood of Christ is to "cleanse our conscience from dead works," so that we may stand uncondemned in the presence of the living God.

Because God accepted Jesus' blood when He carried it into the Heavenly Holy of Holies, He has become by that act the Mediator of the New Covenant.

I Tim. 2:5, "There is one mediator between God and man, Himself man, Christ Jesus."

The reason man needs a mediator is because he has lost his standing with God. He has no ground on which he can approach Him.

Natural man is really an outlaw.

Eph. 2:2 describes his sad condition . . . "Without God and without hope."

Jesus is now to be the Mediator between God and fallen man.

The blood of bulls and goats did not take away sin, it merely covered it temporarily.

But when Christ came, He Redeemed all of those who had trusted in the blood of bulls and goats.

"He died for the redemption of the transgressions that were under the first covenant."

Those sacrifices, under the old covenant, were like a promissory note which He cashed on Calvary.

God kept His covenant with Israel when He sent His Son to become sin, and He laid upon Him all the sins under the First Covenant, that by accepting Him as their Savior Israel might come into the promised Redemption.

HE PUT SIN AWAY

This is the great heart teaching of the book of Hebrews.

Under the First Covenant sin was "covered." The best that the Israelite had under the First Covenant was a blood covering or Atonement.

You remember the word "Atonement" means "to cover."

But under the New Covenant our sins are not covered. They are put away. They are remitted.

They are as though they had never been.

Heb. 9:25-26, "Nor yet that he should be offering himself often, as the high priest entereth into the holy place year by year with blood not his own; else must he often have suffered since the foundation of the world; but now once at the end of the ages hath he been manifested to put away sin by the sacrifice of Himself."

The expression "end of the ages" really means where the two ages met.

The cross was where the old method of counting ended, and it was the place where the new time began.

The thing that stood between man and God was Adam's transgression.

Jesus put that away.

2 Cor. 5:21, "Him who knew no sin God made to become sin."

Jesus settled the sin problem, made it possible for God to legally remit all that we have ever done, and give to us Eternal Life, making us New Creations.

2 Cor. 5:17-18, "Wherefore if any man is in Christ, he is a new creature; the old things are passed away; behold, they are become new. But all things are of God, who reconciled us to Himself through Christ, and gave unto us the ministry of reconciliation."

Chapter Eleven

THE ONE SACRIFICE

The changing of the Covenant and the changing of the Priesthood left Israel almost homeless.

To leave the gorgeous temple for street preaching, and preaching in grove and cottage meetings was an innovation that almost staggers one.

The one sacrifice that Jesus made ended the slaughtering of animals, the carrying of blood into the Holy of Holies.

It was the end of sin covering.

"He when He had offered one sacrifice for sins forever, sat down on the right hand of the Majesty on High."

This "once for all" offering ended the scape goats bearing away sin.

You must read Lev. 16:1-22 carefully in order to get the picture of the great day of Atonement and the scapegoat.

This was the annual day of humiliation and expiation for the sins of the nation, when the high priest made the atonement for the sanctuary, the priests, and the people.

The high priest, laying aside his official ornaments, first offered a sin-offering for himself and for the priesthood, entering into the Holy of Holies with the blood.

He afterward took two he-goats for the nation. One was slain for Jehovah. On the head of the other the sins of the people were typically laid; it was made the sin-bearer of the nation; and laden with guilt, it was sent away into the wilderness.

Mark 15:38 tells of the death of Jesus and the rending of the veil between the Holy place and the Holy of Holies where the blood was carried and sprinkled upon the Mercy Seat.

This was the end of the Holy of Holies on earth.

It was the beginning of a New Covenant in His Blood.

Acts 20:28 tells us that this was the blood of God.

Heb. 9:12, He had carried this blood of Deity into the Holy of Holies in the New Tabernacle, not made with hands, in the heavens.

It was what He called the "once for all" sacrifice.

Chapter Twelve

THE PRESENT MINISTRY OF CHRIST

The present ministry of Christ has been neglected by most Christians. So many, when they think of His giving His life for us think only of His death and Resurrection.

They do not know that when He sat down on the Father's right hand, that He began to live for us in as much reality as He had died for us.

He is no longer the lowly man of Galilee. He is not the Son made Sin for us, forsaken of God.

He is the Lord of all. He has conquered Satan, sin and disease. He has conquered death.

He possesses all authority in Heaven and in earth. Matt. 28:18.

We can act fearlessly upon His Word, because He stands back of it . . . He is the Surety of it.

He is the Surety of this New Covenant. Heb. 7:22.

JESUS, OUR HIGH PRIEST

The High Priest of the Old Covenant was a type of Christ, the High Priest of the New Covenant.

Once every year the High Priest under the Old Covenant had entered into the tabernacle on earth with the blood of bulls and goats to make a yearly atonement for the sins of Israel. Read Heb. 9:25, 10:1-4.

The priests stood daily, ministering and offering the same sacrifices for the sins of Israel. Heb. 10:11.

Christ entered into Heaven itself with His own blood, having obtained eternal redemption for us.

When God accepted the blood of Jesus Christ, He signified that the claims of Justice had been met, and that man could be legally taken from Satan's authority and restored to fellowship with Himself.

By the sacrifice of Himself, Christ had put sin away.

By the sacrifice of Himself, He had sanctified man.

To sanctify means to "set apart," "to separate." He had separated man from Satan's kingdom and family.

When Christ met Mary after His Resurrection, (John 20:17) He said to her, "Touch me not, for I am not yet ascended unto the Father."

He was then on His way to the Father with His own blood, the token of the penalty He had paid, and He could not be touched by human hands.

Jesus' ministry as High Priest did not end with His carrying His blood into the Holy Place, but He is still the minister of the Sanctuary. Heb. 8:2.

The word, "Sanctuary" in the Greek means "Holy Things."

He is ministering in the "Holy Things." These "Holy Things" are our prayers and worship.

We do not always know how to worship Him as we ought, but He takes our ofttimes crude petitions and worship and makes them beautiful to the Father.

Every prayer, every worship is accepted by the Father when it is presented in the Name of Jesus.

He is a merciful and faithful High Priest. He can be touched with the feelings of our infirmities. Heb. 4:14-16.

He is High Priest forever. Heb. 6:20.

JESUS, THE MEDIATOR

When Christ sat down at the Father's right hand, He had satisfied the claims of Justice, and He became the Mediator between God and man.

Jesus is man's mediator for two reasons: because of what He is, and because of what He has done.

First, Jesus is man's mediator by virtue of what He is . . . He is the union of God and man.

He is the One who existed on an equality with God, made in the likeness of men. Phil. 2:8, 9.

He has bridged the gulf between God and man. He is equal with God, and He is equal with man.

He can represent humanity before God.

This however, was not a sufficient ground for a mediation between God and man. Man was an eternal criminal before God. Man was alienated from God, and under the judgment of Satan.

This brings us to our second fact. Jesus is man's mediator because of what He has done.

Col. 1:22, "Yet now hath He reconciled in the body of His flesh through death, to present you holy, and without blemish and unreprovable through Him."

2 Cor. 5:18, "Who reconciled us unto Himself through Christ."

There could have been no mediator between God and man if there had not been first a Reconciliation made between God and man.

Man was unrighteous in His condition of spiritual death. While he was in that condition, He could not approach God.

Neither could any Mediator have approached God for him.

Christ has reconciled us unto God through His death on the cross, so that He now presents man holy and without blemish before God. Therefore, man has a right to approach God through Christ, his mediator.

From the fall of man until Jesus sat down at God's right hand, no man had ever approached God except over a bleeding sacrifice, through a Divinely appointed priesthood, or by an angelic visitation or dream.

On the ground of His High Priestly offering of His own blood, He perfected our Redemption, He satisfied the claims of justice and made it possible for God to legally give man Eternal Life, making him righteous, and giving him a standing as a Son.

He is the Mediator of the New Covenant. Heb. 9:15.

Jesus is seated. He is the High Priestly Mediator that is to introduce lost men to God.

Man has no approach now but through the new Mediator.

By one sacrifice He has put sin away, and by one act He carried His blood into the Holy of Holies.

By that one act Heb. 10:19 declares that all can now enter boldly through the veil into the very presence of the Father and stand there without condemnation.

I would that we were able to make the church understand this blessed truth.

There is so much sin-consciousness, and so little consciousness of the Finished work of Christ taught.

We hear Him cry, Heb. 4:14-16, "Come boldly to the throne of grace and find a blessing to meet every need."

It seems to me as though the Master were saying, "Stop your crying, stop your groaning, come with joy to the throne of love gifts and let me fill your basket with blessings."

Heb. 10:12-13 tells us that one sacrifice of His own blood now in the presence of the Father, on the Mercy Seat, has made all this available to those who take Christ as Savior and Lord.

His work is finished. In the Father's mind our Redemption is complete.

JESUS, THE INTERCESSOR

Jesus, as High Priest, carried His blood into the Holy of Holies, satisfying the claims of Justice that were against natural man.

As Mediator, He introduces the unsaved man to God.

John 14:6, Jesus is the way to God, and no one can approach God except through Him. As soon as man accepts Christ he becomes a child of God. Then Christ begins His intercessory work for him.

Jesus is Mediator for the sinner, but He is intercessor for the Christian.

The first question that comes to us is: "Why does the child of God need someone to intercede for him?

We can find the answer to that in Rom. 12:2.

At the New Birth, our spirits receive the life of God. The next need is that our minds be renewed.

Before we came into the Family, we walked as natural men . . . Satan-ruled men. Satan ruled our minds.

Now that our spirits have received the life of God, our minds must be renewed so that we will know our privileges and responsibilities as children of God.

The New Birth is instantaneous, but the renewing of our mind is a gradual process. Its growth is determined by our study and meditation on the Word.

During this period we need the intercession of Christ.

Many times we strain our fellowship with the Father, as in our ignorance of His will, we many times say and do things that are not pleasing to Him.

Then again, we need His intercession because of demoniacal persecution against us.

Demons persecute us for righteousness' sake. They hate and fear us because God has declared us righteous.

Because we have not fully learned of our authority they cause us to stumble many times.

Regardless of this, He is able to save us to the uttermost, because He ever lives to pray for us. Heb. 7:25.

No one can lay anything to the charge of God's child. God has declared him righteous. There is no one to condemn him. Jesus is living to make intercession for him. Rom. 8:33-34.

JESUS, THE ADVOCATE

We came to the Father through Christ, our Mediator.

We have felt the sweet influence of His Intercession on our behalf. Now we want to know Him as our Advocate before the Father.

Many Christians today, who are living in broken fellowship, would be living victorious lives in Christ if they knew that Jesus was their Advocate.

Because of our unrenewed minds and Satanic persecution, we sometimes sin and cause our fellowship with the Father to be broken.

Every child of God who breaks fellowship with the Father is under condemnation. If he had no advocate to plead his case before the Father he would be in a sad position.

The Word shows us that if we do sin we have an advocate with the Father.

Consider the meaning of the word "advocate." In Webster's dictionary we read: "One who pleads the cause of another in a court of law; one who defends, vindicates, or espouses a cause by argument; an upholder; a defender; one summoned to aid."

Christ is our defender, our upholder. He is always there, at the right hand of God, ready to come to our aid . . . to intercede on our behalf.

I John 2:1, "My little children, these things I write unto you that ye may not sin, and if any man sins we have an advocate with the Father, Jesus Christ, the Righteous."

In I John 1:3-9 is God's method for maintaining our fellowship with Him. If we sin so that our fellowship is broken, we may renew that fellowship by confessing our sin.

He is unable to act as our advocate unless we confess our sins. The moment we confess them He takes up our case before the Father.

The Word declares that when we confess our sins, He is righteous and faithful to forgive us our sins and to cleanse us from all unrighteousness . . . to wipe them out as though they had never been.

47

It is absolutely essential that Christians know Jesus as their advocate. Many who are out of fellowship have confessed their sins many times without receiving a sense of restoration, because they did not know Jesus was their Advocate. They did not take forgiveness when they confessed their sins. They did not act upon the Word which declared that the Father forgives the moment they confess.

No Christian should ever remain in broken fellowship any longer than it takes to ask forgiveness.

What the Father forgives He forgets. A child of His should never dishonor His Word by ever thinking of his sins again.

JESUS, THE SURETY

Jesus is our personal surety. This is the most vital of all the ministries of Jesus at the Father's right hand.

Under the Old Covenant, the High Priest was the surety. If he failed, it interrupted the relationship between God and Israel. The blood of the atonement lost its efficacy.

Under the New Covenant, Jesus is the High Priest and the Surety of the New Covenant.

Our position before the Father is absolutely secure. We know that throughout our lifetime we have at the right hand of God a Man who is there for us.

He is representing us before the Father.

He always has a standing with the Father.

Always, regardless of our standing, we have one representing us before the Father.

Our position is secure.

Chapter Thirteen

THREE BIG WORDS
"REMISSION"

This is one of the great words of the New Covenant.

It means wiping out as though it had never been. When an army is disbanded, it is remitted . . . it stops being.

When God remits our sins, they are wiped out as though they had never been.

The word "remission" is never used but in connection with the New Birth.

After we become Christians, then we have our sins forgiven on the basis of our relationship and the intercession of Christ.

When we come to Him as sinners, and take Christ as Savior, confess Him as our Lord, then all that we have ever done is wiped out.

In the New Birth all that we have ever been stops being and a New Creation takes the place of the old.

Six or eight times the word "remission" is translated "forgiveness" in the Epistles.

Eph. 1:7 "In whom we have our Redemption through His blood, the remission of our trespasses."

Read also Col. 1:13-14; Luke 24:47; Acts 2:38; Acts 26:18; Acts 10:43.

The remission of our sins takes the place of the scapegoat under the First Covenant.

It bore away their sins once a year, while the blood covered Israel as a nation.

On the basis of the blood of Christ, our sins are remitted and we are re-created.

"FORGIVENESS"

Forgiveness is a relationship word.

I am speaking now from a New Covenant point of view.

When the sinner accepts Christ as Savior, his spirit is re-created, his sins are remitted, but being ignorant, he will always be conscious of sin.

On the ground of his relationship as a child of God, and Jesus' ministry at the right hand of the Father, there is ground for forgiveness for any sin that he commits.

I John 1 and 2 deals with this great issue of forgiveness.

When a child of God commits sin, he breaks his fellowship with the Father.

He does not break his relationship. He merely breaks the fellowship, just as a husband and wife do when they say an unkind word. It destroys the fellowship of the home, but that can be restored by asking forgiveness.

We are so constituted that we can forgive.

The same holds true between a Christian and the Father.

The moment that we sin and fellowship with the Father is broken, if we confess our sins He is faithful and righteous to forgive us our sins and to cleanse us from all unrighteousness.

I John 2:1-2, "My little children, these things I write unto you that ye may not sin. And if any man sin, we have an advocate with the Father, Jesus Christ the righteous."

That remarkable expression "the righteous" holds wrapped within it marvelous Grace.

"ATONEMENT"

The First Covenant had law, which we call the Mosaic Law, the priesthood, sacrifices, and the ordinances.

When the law was broken (as it had to be because Israel was spiritually dead) the priesthood was ordered to make an atonement, or a covering, for them.

They did not have Eternal Life. That could not come until Jesus came and redeemed us. He said, "I am come that ye might have life, and have it abundantly."

You remember that receiving Eternal Life is the greatest event in any human being's experience.

On the great day of Atonement we see two remarkable things that take place.

First, surrounded by great precautions, the high priest carries the blood of an innocent animal into the holy of holies and sprinkles it upon the mercy seat that covers the broken law.

Now Israel is blood covered for one year.

Lev. 17:11 tells us that the blood is given as a covering, or atonement, by reason of the life that is in it.

It is the life of an innocent animal typically spread over spiritually dead Israel.

The next fact is the scapegoat. Aaron lays the sins of Israel upon the head of the scapegoat which is led away into the wilderness to be devoured by wild beasts.

For a year, they are free, blood covered, and their sins are borne away.

Chapter Fourteen

THE FOURFOLD BLESSINGS

There are fourfold blessings of the Covenant.

The first blessing that comes with the Covenant is the Righteousness that God imparts to every member of the New Covenant.

When you accept Jesus Christ as your Savior, the moment you are born again, that moment God imparts to you Righteousness.

That gives you a standing in the presence of the Father identical with the standing of Jesus.

We have never known it. We shrink from it.

After a little while it is going to take possession of you, you are going to see it and there will be men and women who will rise up and act like Jesus.

He had no consciousness of inferiority before the Father, for He had no consciousness of sin.

If you actually believe the Bible, and believe that God is your Righteousness, and that you are a New Creation, created in Christ Jesus, you will have no sense of sin.

He has put sin away by the sacrifice of Himself, and the only consciousness you will ever have of sin is when you do something that is not right; and then you will take advantage of the Blood of Christ and of the advocacy of Jesus.

Ever since the Lutheran proclamation we have done one thing! We have magnified sin, we have preached the devil, we have preached our own wickedness and our own unrighteousness, and we have kept it before the people so continuously that no preacher or layman dares think of himself except in the terms of a poor weak worm of the dust!

You know what the evangelists have done. They have come into a church, they want to get results, so they preach so as to bring the whole congregation under condemnation and get them to the altar in order to get a reputation as an evangelist.

We have absolutely taught unbelief! We have taught everything but the gospel of Christ.

What is the Gospel?

The Gospel is this: that God, on the ground of the substitutionary sacrifice of Jesus Christ, is able to declare that He is righteous, and that He Himself is our righteousness, the moment we believe on Jesus.

This is the most staggering thing the mind ever grasped... that God Almighty becomes your righteousness the moment you believe on the Lord Jesus Christ.

When you learn to walk as Jesus walked, without any consciousness of inferiority to God or Satan, you will have faith that will absolutely stagger the world!

Do you know what hinders our faith today?

We go before the Lord, BUT we listen to the devil before we go there. We go there with a sense of inferiority, the devil's message ringing in our ears!

Christians as a whole are afraid of Satan, dare not say they are free, dare not face Satan.

God's Righteousness makes you fearless in Satan's presence.

We rob the work of Jesus Christ of its efficacy, and we stand powerless before the adversary because we have doubted the integrity of the Word of God.

God's righteousness has been imparted to you, not as an "experience," but as a legal fact.

This is the most tremendous truth that God has given us in the Pauline Revelation, and this is the very heart of the New Covenant, that God makes us like Himself.

Weren't you made in His image and likeness?

That image is an image of righteousness.

If God declares that you are righteous, what business have you to condemn yourself?

Another blessing that this covenant brings is your union with God.

When those two men drank each other's blood, they became one, absolutely one.

When Abraham and God cut the covenant, they became one.

"I am the vine and ye are the branches."

Are you a partner of Christ? Do you dwell in Christ? Does Christ dwell in you?

Paul said, "It is no longer I that live, but Christ liveth in me." Gal. 2:20.

The Incarnation was God becoming one with us.

The Blood Covenant made Paul disown himself and utterly own Christ as his life. It made Christ leave Glory and come here to be one with us.

Now you can stand as fearlessly in the presence of hell, in

the presence of the devil, as you would in the presence of some little inferior thing.

Didn't Jesus meet him and conquer him for us? Didn't He strip him of his authority? Didn't He take his armor from him, and didn't He leave him paralyzed?

Greater is He that is in us than the devil.

Why should we be afraid of him?

Why not stand before the world as a conqueror?

You are in blood covenant relationship with God Almighty.

When you were born again you entered the Covenant.

Let me give you a picture.

You remember the mighty men of David. They were types of Christians. One of those men slew 800 men in personal combat in a single day.

He said, "One shall chase a thousand, and two put ten thousand to flight."

Blood Covenant men!

As long as David walked with God in the covenant, not one of his warriors were ever slain.

Are you a partaker of the Divine nature? Yes.

Are you a son of God? Yes.

Has God given you His righteousness? Yes.

Is God your righteousness? Certainly.

Then, has He given you a legal right to the use of Jesus' Name? Certainly.

Do you see what kind of a man you are?

You are not a weakling. You stand like the Son of God. You are a son of God.

Now the only thing is this: we have to overcome the effect of these false teachings:

For generations they have made us sinners, and they have talked to us as sinners.

Almost every one of the old hymns start beautifully, but before they finish we are just poor weaklings, and we are living in sin, and we are under bondage, and they have kept us there.

Christ is almost unknown to us.

THE OBJECT OF THIS REVELATION

What is the object of this revelation? To let us know what we really are in Jesus Christ.

You say, "That is all right, Dr. Kenyon, but if you only knew how weak I am . . ."

What does He say?

What is the argument and conclusion of the Book of Hebrews?

"Looking unto Jesus, the author and finisher of our faith."

Just as long as you look at yourself you don't amount to anything; you are just like Peter.

When he started to walk with Jesus on the waves, he didn't sink; but the moment he looked at the boisterous waves, that moment he sank.

You are linked up to God Almighty.

"These things have I written unto you that believe on the name of the Son of God; that ye may know that ye have eternal life." I John 5:13.

That gives you your legal standing before God, gives you your place in the covenant.

I say it reverently, if I understand the Gospel of the Lord Jesus Christ, this is the vision He has given me of it: that all of heaven's ability and heaven's glory and heaven's strength are at the disposal of the believer.

This is the most miraculous thing the world ever saw.

I believe that in the last days there is going to be an unveiling of the power of God, and multitudes will arise and live.

Weymouth's translation of Romans 5:17 tells us that we reign as Kings in the Realm of Life in Christ.

We are to absolutely reign as Christ, and with Christ.

How? By faith.

HIS CHALLENGE TO US

Is God your righteousness?

You say, "I am trying to make Him my righteousness."

Can you make Him your righteousness?

If you believe on Jesus Christ, He IS your righteousness.

Then go out and act it. Dare to let God loose in you.

Chapter Fifteen

REDEMPTION IS BY GOD

With the horrible picture in view of Satan's finished work, our hearts cry out: "Who is able, who has the ability to meet man's need in a plight like this?"

Thank God, there is an answer.

When God saw the condition of man, He began immediately to make provision for his redemption.

He knew that man could not redeem himself; He knew that man had no ability to approach Him.

So, God gave first the Abrahamic Covenant.

Then, with the Abrahamic Covenant, when Abraham's descendants became a nation, He gave to them the Law of the Covenant, the priesthood of the Covenant, the atonement of the Covenant, and the sacrifices and offerings of the Covenant.

All these were given to prepare a people.

Out of that people was to come the Incarnate God-Man, and that Incarnate God-Man was to break:

First: The power of Satan and redeem man from his bondage, and restore to man his righteousness so he could stand in the Father's presence on as good a footing, if not better, than Adam had before the fall, thus taking from man all the sense of his guilt and his sin.

Second: Satan's dominion, to redeem man so absolutely, to shatter Satan's dominion so completely that the weakest bondman of the Devil could become a participator in this restored righteousness, so that man could live a life of victory over this old age-ruler, Satan.

This God-Man, this Incarnate One, was to make such a

complete and perfect sacrifice that God could not only legally restore to man his lost righteousness and give to man his perfect redemption, but could also do the mightiest things that beggar the very imagination of man, make man a New Creation.

What?

Yes, sir! He absolutely makes man a New Creation, imparts His own nature to man, and drives out that cringing fear nature, sin nature, Satan nature.

The big, glorious, wonderful nature of God takes its place until we stand in the presence of God, under the blazing light of His grace and love.

We open up as a rose does to the sun, until the fulness of His love comes flooding into our beings and then flows back again to Him, our own wonderful Father. We are His own beloved children.

Reader, you are standing in the presence of the Miracle of Miracles, the grace of God that is restoring the lost human race, swinging it back out of the orbit of selfishness and weakness and fear into the realm of faith, love and life of God.

He not only will legally restore righteousness, legally redeem us, legally make us a New Creation, but He can also legally give the Holy Spirit to every one of the New Creation.

That great, mighty Spirit that raised up Jesus from the dead can actually come into these bodies of ours and make them His home, until the heart whispers, then sings, and then breaks into the anthem, "Greater is He that is in me, than he that is in the world."

On the wings of that anthem we move up out of the reason realm and soar by faith into the realm of love where faith rules and where Jesus is Lord.

He not only did this, but He gave to us the legal right to use His Name so that we may cast out Satan, lay hands on the sick so they become well, and defeat the very purposes of Satan.

Oh, we have that Name. That Name makes us just like Jesus.

When you live in that Name and walk in that Name, the Devil cannot tell you from Jesus.

You look like Him. You are clothed in His righteousness; you are filled with His life.

You have His Name stamped upon you.

Ah, but He did more than that.

He gave to us the Revelation. We call it the Word, and this Word is the Word of the Spirit.

That great mighty Spirit that raised Jesus from the dead has come into you.

Now, through human lips, the Holy Spirit wields that Word and conquers the vast armies of hell.

You are the very Son of God, called into fellowship with Jesus Christ, with restored righteousness, restoreth liberty and freedom, a New Creation indwelt of the Holy Spirit, with the living Word of God.

You have a fellowship richer than Adam ever dreamed of.

And this body that Satan made mortal, when Jesus comes will receive immortality and never die again.

Death can never threaten us and fill us with fear.

We stand complete in all the fullness of His completeness now.

What will it be when the pearly gates unfold, and we, His love-subjects, His love-slaves, and His redeemed forever, behold our Lord seated upon the throne of the ages.

Chapter Sixteen

BENEATH HIS FEET

This is the climax of the Redemptive work of Christ.

Eph. 1:19-23, We have seen Jesus after the Resurrection exalted to the highest seat in the universe, with all dominion, all authority, all power beneath His feet.

We know in Col. 1:18, we are His feet, His body.

All that is beneath His feet is beneath ours.

His victory is our victory.

There is no reason for Christ's coming and entering the tremendous contest for our Redemption unless it was for us.

He did not do it for Himself. What He did for us is ours.

What is ours requires nothing but the taking.

God did not do this work, then lock it up and keep it away from us and dole it out to a few.

In His Redemption there is a perfect Righteousness given us. 2 Cor. 5:21.

That Righteousness permits us to come boldly to the throne of Grace.

That Righteousness permits us to enjoy the fulness of our rights in Christ.

That Righteousness is based on Rom. 4:25 and Rom. 5:1 "Being therefore Justified on the ground of Faith, we have peace with God through our Lord Jesus Christ."

Through His work on the Cross and His death and Resurrection, He made peace.

He arose, because He had conquered our enemies.

He had put to naught those who had held us in bondage.

Col. 2:15, "He put off from Himself the principalities and the powers and made a show of them openly."

We know that the Father planned our Redemption. John 3:16.

Jesus carried out that plan. Eph. 1:7; I Pet. 2:24.

John 6:47, "Verily, verily, I say unto you, He that believeth hath eternal life."

I believe that the plan was carried out, and that I have Eternal Life; that "By His stripes I am healed"; by His Grace I am more than a conqueror.

I John 5:13 declares that I have Eternal Life.

If I have Eternal Life, I have my healing.

(For a complete exposition of healing in the Plan of Redemption, send for our book, "Jesus the Healer." Thousands have been healed while reading this book.)

I have every need supplied so that I can do all things in Christ who strengthens me.

There is no struggle, no long agonizing prayer, no need of fasting to get it.

It is mine!

Eph. 1:3 says He has blessed me with every spiritual blessing.

How do I get it?

I just thank Him for it.

Thanksgiving throws the door open wide, Praise keeps it open.

For years we have been taught that we had to groan and struggle and cry and pray and "hold on" to get the answer.

All that is the work of unbelief, and grows out of our ignorance of the Word and of our rights in Christ.

If I Cor. 3:21 is true, that "All things are ours"; and Col. 2:10, "We are complete in Him"; and Eph. 1:22, "All things are beneath our feet"; and Satan has been conquered; and we are more than victors through Him who loved us; where is the place for begging and crying?

It dishonors the Father.

Chapter Seventeen

"IN MY NAME"

We are entering into the era of dominion linked with Omnipotence, filled with Him who is greater than he that is in the world, with the wisdom of Him who spoke a universe into being, and with a legal right to use His Name in every crisis of our lives.

John 14:13-14, "And whatsoever ye shall ask in my name, that will I do, that the Father may be glorified in the Son."

This is not prayer. The promise of the use of His Name in prayer is given in the 15th and 16th chapters.

It is what Peter used at the beautiful gate of the temple as recorded in Acts 3.

He used the Name. He said, "In the Name of Jesus Christ of Nazareth, walk."

That man who had been lame from birth leaped to his feet, perfectly well and strong.

Jesus said, "Whatsoever ye shall demand in my Name (for the word ask means demand) I will do it."

A woman once came to me with a cancer of the breast. It had been a running sore for a year and a half. She had suffered constant excruciating pain.

In the Name of Jesus I commanded that cancer to stop being. The next day she came back and said the cancer was gone. There was no more pain.

Another with a fibroid tumor that was cancerous in its nature came. The Name of Jesus healed it.

Cases of Tuberculosis, Arthritis and Cancer are defeated by the use of the Name. No disease nor infirmity can stand against the Name.

"In my Name they shall cast out demons."

There is no prayer about that, that is where we come to this bound and afflicted man or woman and say, "In the Name of Jesus, Satan we charge you to leave this body, take every demon with you and go back to Hell where you belong!"

Satan knows he is defeated, and when we use the Name he must leave.

John 15:16, "That whatsoever ye shall ask of the Father in my Name, He may give it you."

This is prayer.

You remember the word "ask" in the Greek means "demand."

You are not demanding it of God. You are demanding that forces that are injurious shall be broken, that diseases shall be healed, that circumstances shall be changed, that money shall come.

Jesus is going to look after this thing that you demand in His Name.

Read carefully John 16:24-27 and you will catch a glimpse of your legal right to use the Name of Jesus.

"Hitherto you have asked nothing in my name. Ask and ye shall receive that your joy may be made full."

You have noticed the absence of the word "believe" or the word "faith."

In all three of these wonderful chapters with these great promises, the words "faith" or "believe" do not occur.

We are in the family, and because we are in the family we have a legal right to these things.

Eph. 1:3 illustrates it, "Blessed be the God and Father of

our Lord Jesus Christ, who hath blessed us with every spiritual blessing in the heavenly places in Christ."

What Jesus did was for us.

"HOW TO USE THE NAME"

This is the most vital truth to every one of us. How I have studied this problem.

The Name of Jesus is used in two major ways. First, in prayer to the Father.

John 15:16, "And whatsoever ye shall ask of the Father in my name He may give it you."

John 16:23, "If ye shall ask anything of the Father in my name He will give it to you."

Prayer is to be made to the Father, in Jesus' Name, not to the Holy Spirit or Jesus. This is Divine order.

Your judgment or my judgment or any other man's opinion is of no value.

"When you pray, say our Father." Jesus stands between us and the Father in His mediatorial, High Priestly ministry to make it good.

He declares that whatsoever we ask in that Name the Father will give it to us. That is final. That is absolute.

John 14:13-34 He tells us how to use the Name of Jesus in sickness or in adverse circumstances, or any other crisis.

This is the way I use the Name: Here is a case of T.B. I lay my hands on him and say, "In the Name of Jesus Christ, body obey the Word. The Word declares that 'by His stripes you are healed,' I command you, spirit of T.B. to leave this body now."

The demon of sickness leaves, and the person is healed.

"USING THE NAME TODAY"

You wonder why the Church does not use this Name today.

Satan has kept our eyes blinded to its use.

Here in the city of Seattle hardly any of the churches are using this Name in their daily life. The sick are taken to the hospital or attended by doctors.

It is a remarkable fact that in our own congregation we have practically no sickness. If there is any, they pray for each other and are immediately healed.

Acts 4:13-22 is the story of the trial of Peter and John for healing that helpless man with the Name of Jesus.

"And seeing the man that was healed standing with them they could say nothing against it . . . but that it spread no further among the people they threatened them not to speak henceforth in this name."

Why?

They did not object to the resurrection being taught, or to the New Birth being taught.

But, they objected to the teaching in the Name because there was the power of healing in that Name.

Hebrews 13:8 declares that Jesus Christ is the same yesterday, today and forever.

There is just as much power in that name as there ever was. It is not a problem of faith, it is a problem of your daring to lay hands upon the sick and see them recover.

It is a problem of your daring to pray to the Father in that name, and miracles will be the result of that prayer.

Stand on your Blood Covenant rights. Dare to use the Name!

Chapter Eighteen

WHAT THE LORD'S TABLE TEACHES

There are two outstanding characteristics of the Father and Jesus. They are more than characteristics, they are a part of Themselves.

God is love. Not only is He a love God, but He is a Father God. He believed the universe into being. When man went astray, He believed that He could bring him back, that a challenge of love would reach him.

He believed men into New Creations, and He believes them into victory. He believes them into the love walk with each other.

God is a Father God; Jesus is like His Father. He was the introducer of love to the world.

Jesus came to introduce His Father, and His Father is love. It was an introduction to a new kind of love to the broken, wrecked human race.

Love is the only universal appeal to man. Love is an appeal to his heart. Faith is an appeal to his imagination, but love is the real appeal.

Jesus so loved that He poured out His life for us.

Jesus believed as the Father believed. Jesus acted His faith. He believed that if He became man's substitute, that man would respond, that if He could prove to the world that He loved men so much that He died for them, that He suffered the torments of the damned for them, there would be a response.

He acted His faith. He has faith in humanity today. He has faith in the church. He has faith in Himself and in His own living Word that it would win out.

He has faith in love.

The Lord's table is a confession of our faith and our loyalty to love, just as the Father's giving Jesus is a confession of His love. Jesus' coming and giving Himself for us was a confession of His love.

They were both loyal to love.

Jesus said these significant words, "As oft as ye eat this bread, and drink this cup, you show forth my death till I come."

It was a Covenant. He said, "This is my blood of the New Covenant." As often as you drink it, you show your faith in His Covenant until He comes.

When you eat the bread, and drink the cup, you ratify this Covenant. It is a love Covenant.

First, it is your loyalty and love to Jesus. Second, it is your loyalty and love for His Body, the Church.

It is a confession of your love one for another. It is a confession that you have eaten and drunk with them, and now you are going to bear their burdens.

You have identified yourself with each other, just as He identified Himself with you in His Incarnation and Substitution.

That would be the Master's attitude toward the Lord's table.

When I break the bread and drink the cup, I not only confess my loyalty to Him, but to every member of the Body of Christ who breaks that bread and drinks that cup with me.

If I am strong, I bear the burdens of the weak. I have taken over their weaknesses.

The Lord's Table means that I will never criticize, but I will assume their spiritual responsibilities and weaknesses.

THE NEED OF THE HOUR

Some one is going to rise and understand this.

Some body of people is going to enter into it.

I have a conviction that this is the eleventh hour message, that this is the message for the Church today.

In the troubled days that lie ahead, we are going to require all that God can give us, and be to us, to stand the tests we are going through . . . and will go through.

You see, brethren, this blood covenant teaching, this relationship teaching, this ability to use the Name of Jesus, this marvelous teaching of our identification and our privileges, is the message for the coming days. It will fit us to meet the very forces of darkness.

Do you know that Jesus, in the Great Commission in the Gospel of Mark, did a peculiar thing?

He said, "In My Name ye shall cast out demons."

I had not seen its significance. I know now what it means. In the last days demons are going to become very prominent.

Satan, knowing that his days are shortened, is coming to the earth with all his host, and we are going to pass into a period of spiritual conflict such as the church has never known.

This will not only be persecution, but it will be demons breaking and crushing the spirit of the church in the individual.

The church must learn the secret of standing against the hosts of darkness in the NAME.

THE BLOOD COVENANT

I've a right to grace, in the hardest place,
  On the ground of the Blood Covenant;
I've a right to peace that can never cease,
  On the ground of the Blood Covenant.

I've a right to joy, that can never cloy,
  On the ground of the Blood Covenant;
I've a right to power, yes, this very hour,
  On the ground of the Blood Covenant.

I've a right to health, thru my Father's wealth,
  On the ground of the Blood Covenant;
I my healing take, Satan's hold must break,
  On the ground of the Blood Covenant.

I've a legal right, now to win this fight,
  On the ground of the Blood Covenant;
I will take my part with courageous heart,
  On the ground of the Blood Covenant.

Now my rights I claim, in His Mighty Name,
  On the ground of the Blood Covenant;
And my prayers prevail, tho all Hell assail,
  On the ground of the Blood Covenant.

On the ground of the Blood,
  On the ground of the Blood Covenant;
I will claim my rights, tho the enemy fights,
  On the ground of the Blood Covenant.

E. W. Kenyon.

Inspiring Books
by E. W. KENYON

THE BIBLE IN THE LIGHT
OF OUR REDEMPTION
    A Basic Bible Course

ADVANCED BIBLE COURSE
    Studies in the Deeper Life

PERSONAL EVANGELISM COURSE

THE HIDDEN MAN OF THE HEART

WHAT HAPPENED
    From the Cross to the Throne

NEW CREATION REALITIES

IN HIS PRESENCE
    The Secret of Prayer

THE TWO KINDS OF LIFE

THE FATHER AND HIS FAMILY
    The Story of Man's Redemption

THE WONDERFUL NAME OF JESUS
    Our Rights and Privileges in Prayer

JESUS THE HEALER
    Has Brought Healing to Thousands

KENYON'S LIVING POEMS

THE NEW KIND OF LOVE

THE TWO KINDS OF FAITH

THE TWO KINDS OF RIGHTEOUSNESS

THE BLOOD COVENANT

THE TWO KINDS OF KNOWLEDGE

SIGN POSTS ON THE ROAD TO SUCCESS

IDENTIFICATION

Order From:
KENYON'S GOSPEL PUBLISHING SOCIETY
P.O. Box 973, Lynnwood Washington 98046
Web site: www.kenyons.org